BEHIND THE SCENES BIOGRAPHIES

WHAT YOU NEVER KNEW ABOUT CRISTIANO RONALDO

by Martha E. H. Rustad

CAPSTONE PRESS
a capstone imprint

This is an unauthorized biography.

Published by Spark, an imprint of Capstone
1710 Roe Crest Drive, North Mankato, Minnesota 56003
capstonepub.com

Library of Congress Cataloging-in-Publication Data
Names: Rustad, Martha E. H. (Martha Elizabeth Hillman), 1975- author.
Title: What you never knew about Cristiano Ronaldo / by Martha E.H. Rustad
Description: North Mankato, Minnesota : Spark, an imprint of Capstone, [2023] | Series: Behind the scenes biographies | Includes bibliographical references. | Audience: Ages 9-11 | Audience: Grades 4-6 | Summary: "Cristiano Ronaldo is the world's top soccer player. But what happens when he's not scoring on the pitch? High-interest details and bold photos of his fascinating life will enthrall reluctant and struggling readers, while carefully leveled text will leave them feeling confident"— Provided by publisher.
Identifiers: LCCN 2021056980 (print) | LCCN 2021056981 (ebook) | ISBN 9781666356953 (hardcover) | ISBN 9781669040118 (paperback) | ISBN 9781666356960 (pdf) | ISBN 9781666356984 (kindle edition)
Subjects: LCSH: Ronaldo, Cristiano, 1985- —Juvenile literature. | Soccer players—Portugal—Biography—Juvenile literature.
Classification: LCC GV942.7.R626 R87 2023 (print) | LCC GV942.7.R626 (ebook) | DDC 796.334092 [B]—dc23/eng/20220604
LC record available at https://lccn.loc.gov/2021056980
LC ebook record available at https://lccn.loc.gov/2021056981

Editorial Credits
Editor: Erika L. Shores; Designer: Heidi Thompson; Media Researchers: Jo Miller and Pam Mitsakos; Production Specialist: Tori Abraham

Image Credits
Getty Images: JOANA SOUSA/Stringer, 19; Newscom: ASLON2/MEGA/Mirropix, 22, GWGLA/MEGA/Courtesy of NIKE, 28, ZCVA/Supplied by WENN, 26; Shutterstock: Bascar, 25 (bottom), cristiano barni, 12, 13, 16, dimcars, 25 (top), F8 studio, 15, Grisha Bruev, 21, Helle, 20 (bottom), irin-k, 5, Javi Az, 11 (bottom), MDI, 20 (top), Nicolo Campo, 7, 29 (top), Oleh Dubyna, 18, ONYXprj, 23, ph.FAB, Cover, 4, 9, sbonsi, 14, Tofudevil, 24, TotemArt, 29 (bottom), Vlad1988, 10, Yuri Turkov, 11 (top)

All internet sites appearing in back matter were available and accurate when this book was sent to press.

Printed in the United States 5450

TABLE OF CONTENTS

Words in **bold** are in the glossary.

GOAL!

Cristiano Ronaldo scores. He scores with his right foot. He scores with his left foot. He even scores with his head. After he scores, he jumps and spins. He yells out, "Sí!"

Ronaldo has scored a hat trick 58 times. That's three goals in one game. He is one of the world's best soccer players.

RONALDO BY THE NUMBERS

Ronaldo has racked up big numbers! How much do you know about him on and off the pitch?

1. How many goals has he scored in his career?

2. At what age did Ronaldo start playing soccer?

3. How old was Ronaldo when he had a heart problem fixed?

4. How fast can he run?

5. How many pro teams has he played on?

1. Over 800, so far **2.** 8 **3.** 15

4. top speed of 20.2 miles (32.5 kilometers) per hour **5.** 4

Ronaldo's biggest number is his **salary**. In 2021, Manchester United paid him $70 million. How much has he earned over his whole career? More than $1 billion!

70

2021

FACT

Cristiano Ronaldo dos Santos Aveiro is his full name. "Ronaldo" comes from Ronald Reagan. Reagan was the U.S. president in 1985 when Ronaldo was born.

1

ALL HE DOES IS **WIN!**

He scores goals and gold! Ronaldo won the Golden Boot four times. That means he scored the most goals in Europe in a season.

Another golden award is the Golden Ball. FIFA gives this award to the best player of the year. Ronaldo has five Golden Balls.

Teams win trophies with Ronaldo on the pitch. He helped Real Madrid win their 10th European Cup. His team, Manchester United, won the Champions League in Europe. Juventus won the Supercoppa Italia with him on their team. So far, Ronaldo has won 32 trophies during his career.

Jeep
Jeep
Jeep
19

Zero. Surprisingly, that is how many World Cups Ronaldo has won. He wants to win one for Portugal. It is his home country.

Ronaldo's trophies fill his own museum. The CR7 museum is on his home island of Madeira, in Portugal.

FACT

The name CR7 uses his initials along with his **jersey** number.

SO MANY FOLLOWERS

Ronaldo has more social media followers than any other person in the world! His Instagram followers total about 377 million. On Facebook, around 150 million people follow him. He has about 96.1 million Twitter followers.

What does he post about? He shares photos of his teammates. Trophies get hugs and kisses from him. He shows off pictures of his family too.

OFF THE PITCH

Ronaldo and his mother, Maria Dolores

Ronaldo doesn't play soccer all the time. He spends time with his family. He is close to his mother, Maria Dolores. He gave her a Mercedes for Mother's Day one year.

Ronaldo is the youngest in his family. He has two sisters and one brother. His brother, Hugo, runs the CR7 museum.

Hugo and Ronaldo at the CR7 museum

At home, Ronaldo lives with his partner, Georgina Rodríguez. He has five children.

Georgina Rodríguez

FACT

Ronaldo's favorite meal is a dish from Portugal. It is made of codfish, onions, potatoes, and eggs.

Ronaldo owns a home in Málaga, Spain.

Ronaldo owns many houses. His Madeira home is seven stories tall. A soccer pitch is in the yard. It even has a pool on the roof! His vacation home is in Spain. He has a home in England too.

FAST CARS

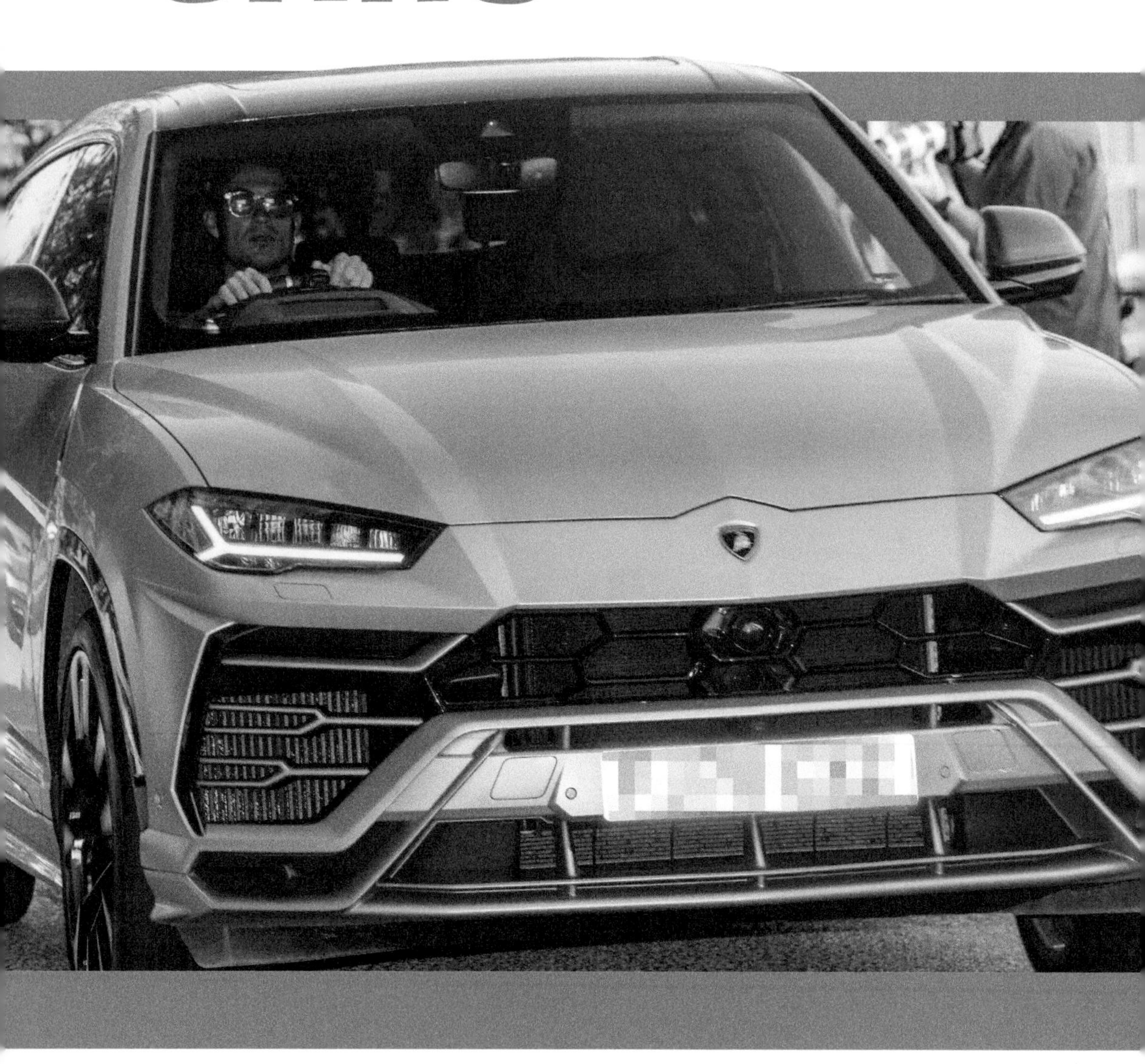

Ronaldo runs fast on the soccer pitch. He also loves to drive fast cars. He owns about 20 sports cars. They are worth around $24 million. One of his favorites? A Rolls-Royce! He has many garages to hold them all.

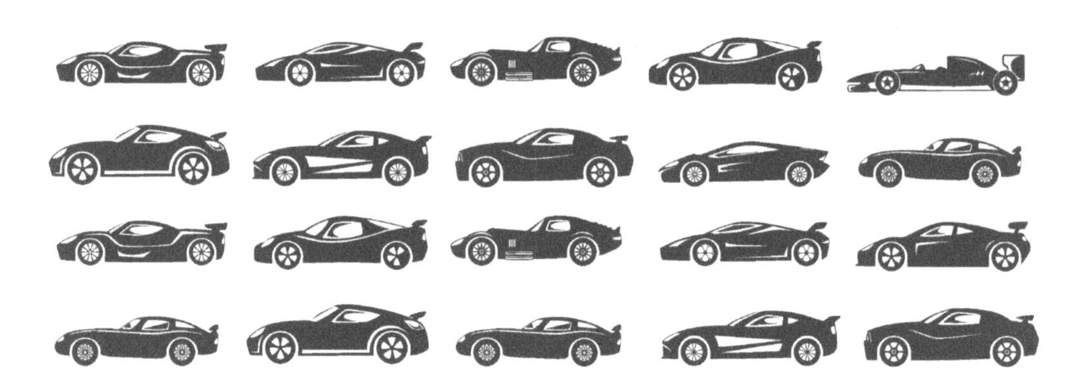

A Bugatti is Cristiano's most expensive car. It cost about $12 million. He also has three other Bugattis, five Ferraris, and a Lamborghini. He even drives a Maserati and a Bentley. For his 35th birthday, Georgina gave him a Mercedes.

A Lamborghini

A Bugatti

A Bugatti

GIVING BACK

Ronaldo is very rich. But he also gives a lot of money away. He gave money to build a **cancer** center at a Madeira hospital. He also gave money to fight COVID-19 in Portugal.

Ronaldo helped raise more than $1 million by selling one of his Golden Boot awards. The money was given to a school charity.

Ronaldo wants kids in Portugal to be able to play soccer like he did. He worked with the Nike company. Together, they rebuilt the soccer pitch where Ronaldo played as a child.

What does Cristiano give that is free? Blood! One donation helps up to three people. He tells other people to give blood too.

Glossary

cancer (KAN-suhr)—a serious disease in which some cells in the body grow faster than normal cells

career (kuh-REER)—a period of time spent in a profession

jersey (JUR-see)—a shirt worn by a team member; each player has a different number

salary (SAL-uh-ree)—the money earned from a job in one year

Read More

Battista, Brianna. *Cristiano Ronaldo*. New York: PowerKids Press, 2019.

Lowe, Alexander. *G.O.A.T. Soccer Strikers*. Minneapolis: Lerner, 2022.

Nicks, Erin. *Cristiano Ronaldo*. Minneapolis: Abdo Publishing, 2020.

Internet Sites

Cristiano Ronaldo Legendary Goals
video.link/w/A2c8c

Premier League: Cristiano Ronaldo
premierleague.com/players/2522/Cristiano-Ronaldo/overview

Real Madrid: Cristiano Ronaldo
realmadrid.com/en/about-real-madrid/history/football-legends/cristiano-ronaldo-dos-santos-aveiro

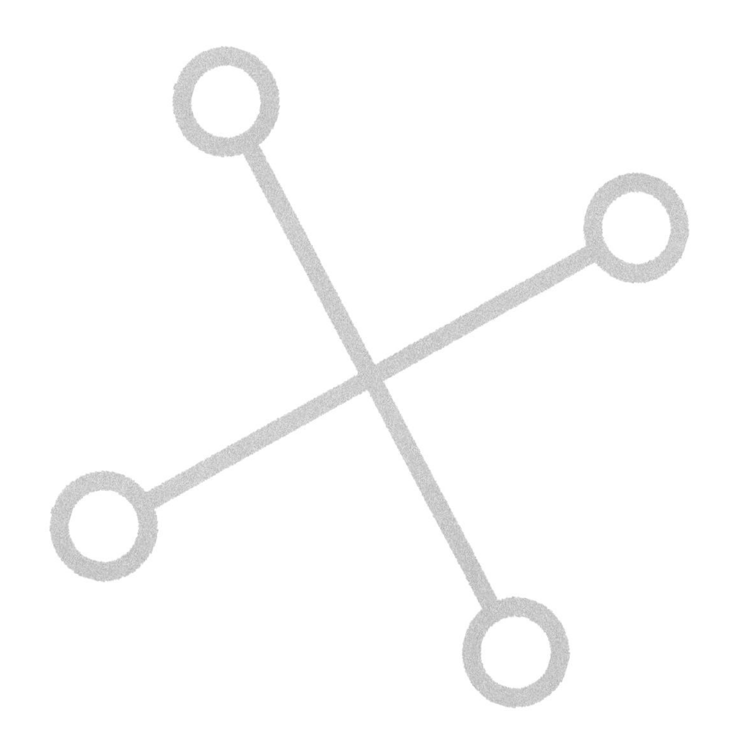

Index

About the Author

Martha E. H. Rustad is the author of more than 300 nonfiction children's books on topics ranging from baby ducks to black holes to ancient Babylon. She lives with her family in Brainerd, Minnesota.